LYNCHBURG

Also by Forrest Gander

Poetry
Rush to the Lake, 1988
Deeds of Utmost Kindness, 1994

Poetry Chapbooks
Eggplants and Lotus Root, 1991
Poetry and Translation (with Carmen Boullosa), 1992

Anthology
*Mouth to Mouth: Poems by Twelve Contemporary Mexican
    Women,* 1993

LYNCHBURG

FORREST GANDER

University of Pittsburgh Press

Pittsburgh • London

The publication of this book is supported by grants from the
National Endowment for the Arts in Washington, D.C., a Federal
agency, and the Pennsylvania Council on the Arts.

Published by the University of Pittsburgh Press, Pittsburgh, Pa.
15260
Copyright © 1993, Forrest Gander
Manufactured in the United States of America
Printed on acid-free paper

Library of Congress Cataloging-in-Publication Data

Gander, Forrest, 1956-
  Lynchburg / Forrest Gander.
      p.   cm.—(Pitt poetry series)
    ISBN 0-8229-3746-8 (alk. paper).—ISBN 0-8229-5498-2 (pbk. :
  alk. paper)
    I. Title. II. Series.
  PS3557.A47L96   1993
  811'.54—dc20   90-62336
                                                        CIP

A CIP catalogue record for this book is available from the British Library.
Eurospan, London

The author and publisher wish to express their grateful acknowledgment to
the following publications in which some of these poems first appeared:
College English, Five Fingers Review, Oblek, Sulfur, TriQuarterly, and *The
William and Mary Review.*

An early version of "Soundtrack and Color Tints" appeared in *The Southern
Review* as "Wisteria Blue."

For Kay Duvernet and Vic Chestnutt,
south of Lynchburg, west of Rome.

Contents

I

Prophecy

If I directed my friends' lives,
I would bring them together.
Each of their lonelinesses would find
I knew them.

Their stories come back, one by one.
Snake doctors flit through the garden.

The porch light shines
And the darkness does not comprehend it.

We stand on the stair to hug,
Kiss one another good night.
I want you to take this.
I have cut it for you.

Also Our Bed Is Green

This poem cannot hold what I have
to fill it. The wax in your ear tastes
bitter until I suck your tongue
and it mixes with the humid trace of my semen.
I have all the tricks of the trade
for overcoming our happiness.

Friends pull up anchor and the heart
tugs its blue moorings.
A turtle is busted apart on rocks
below the dam. Little do we know
the landscape we might pass through
eating sardines and rotten peaches
or how it might mark us
with its fidelity to our words.

Freeze

To the north of Danville,
the thick smoke of sludge fires
rises all night.
Snow like tiny spiders.
The orchard keepers take counsel
and it comes to nothing.
Big rats breeding
in the stacked ricks scare
smaller ones
into the house. Morning:
both traps are sprung.

Soundtrack and Color Tints

There is a pulse so faint
    I have considered
    I imagined it
    beating field, dandelions, and wind.
    It beats mandibles chewing blades
    and the red fiddleback in the attic dark.
While liquid pearls pendulate
    from stalactites
    over blind albinic hellbenders,
        while crawdaddies sift
    through silt, it beats thunderclap, hurricane
    (my own calm is the eye), three periods
    of ho-hum, four interludes of regression.

It beats oil gold,
    chrysophenim, mikado yellow, yolk,
                barium chrome,
    yellow madder, sulfur, tartrazine,
    canary, crocus, saffron, massicot,
              antimony yellow,
    snapdragon, straw in Lynchburg.
    Then: wisteria blue.

                It taps out a thin sheet
    of sound, the light pauses there.

    Defeatist arguments, people who gave up,
    it beats over them. It meters out loss
    until I am small,
        then begins again:

    plum-colored men weighing by their necks,
    President Grant sending clothes and blankets
    from typhoid victims
        to Osage reservations in Missouri.

Silences,
the fires that burn the saved,
days slamming behind one another.
It beats me a half-smoke and I ate it.
It beats the near suicide of Leon Rapollo.
It beats constellated rice pickers
in their endless pitch,
a long evening service
and everyone milling solemnly
through the door, across the grass,
toward the parking lot where the reverend
with a stick and flashlight
scares snakes into shadows
from the warm dust where they have come
                              unloosed.
It beats to the rhythm of a man
    who shovels a pit,
        and digs it, and is fallen into the ditch
            which he made. It beats
                    to the hiss
    of termites swarming the floor
while lovers feigning sleep
    connect points of light

        in the inarticulate heaven and overhear
        through open windows Sheriff Billy Willet's
    drunken, uphill, lisped soliloquy.

Slate-Colored Juncos

Sour newspaper in the oven.
The hounds that none may flee
Have strewn my garbage
In the dark.

Sock feet in galoshes.
Each step crunches and gives. All week,
My three-legged dog
Directs his steaming pizzle
Toward the same
Gilded holes.

Drunk I come
To appreciate
A painting of dock and gull
Hung between heads
Of jackalopes.

Given the afternoon
Off, I stare at things in my room
The length of the afternoon.

Anemic June midnight.
White noise crawling through
The busted streetlight.

Abscess

Good morning kiss. Their teeth glance. Clack of June
bugs against pane. On the porch a young man
in the full sun rocking.
Jars incubate tomato plants. His mother sweeps the dirt
yard away from flowering vinca and bottle tree.
Straightens up, one-eyed by ragged hens. As her boy
ambles away to the steady pulse
in his skull.
The cattle gate
swinging open behind him.
She takes a headache powder
and it is nineteen and twenty seven.
The James overruns its levee, backs up
the Blackwater. Nineteen and twenty nine: she reads his postcard,
the tobacco crop burns. Nineteen and thirty, drought.
Long limp bags drag through fields. The Lord whistles
for the fly. Revival tents threaten a rain
of scorpions. To cure her hiccups,
the woman sees a hypnotist. Promptly
coughs herself to death. In pungs marked men ride. The son
is blown away. No one returns in this story. No one escapes.
The tribe is glued together for ruination, friends.
There is no more time, there is no way out.

Brother

So endeth the evening. Yet
I would like to convince a few people
the clarity of the word *gone*
is a deception. Death remains
noncommittal about the sockdolager.
Albeit, facts reach their vanishing point.
He no longer comes around.
Or uncorks quince wine of an evening, alone.
His grave, a standing trough,
generates a broken wave. So long
to the unshaved face
of a serious and dark-clad company.
The streetlamps blow out behind him.

June the Third

It happens
in the evening
which always comes
solo, like a man through
a bar door, the anniversary
of a death, like
the number of hands
squeezing this shot glass.

Prologue to a Bidding

Though each single life occurs
in a series of occasions
    striking only by what
blurry context
    precedes them—
        So come to know
        what I should have wanted
        to say—from
an internal perspective
there is no series. Only
    event. Music knocks
us down. His brow
        shadowing the guitar player's
    accipitrine eyes. Tile roofs
glistening under rain.
On a dirt road
a resuscitative walk.
        The kite hits
    the copperhead. Cicadas
halt. The air blanks.
    And strangers crane up
    from whatever they are doing
to meet your gaze as you go past,
    thinking, I am with you, I am
                you.

II

Parable in Wolves' Clothing

The house is building a woman.

The witness lies, how it comes easy.

The house claims her nervous system
Will multiply in a season
Out of fire.

She moans,
    He eats, he saws
      My bones in half.

The man tells his story like a witness
Standing on a hill at night court.

He hurls his tenor past the moon
While the night goes pale as teeth.

He curses,
    You will marry a kitten
      And she will bear you a ghost.

While stars gallop from the bush
He bleeds. His face matted

With cold smoke.

She lays her fire in.

They lift the trapdoor from the night.

Cockeye

You are strikingly undone
Like a car with one headlight
Mistaken for the moon
Over Bedford Virginia
The province of singing frogs
I would like to stroke your fine white belly

Or you undress yourself
With your own eyes
On whose surface every light breaks
That has traveled through anniversaries of darkness
Inside you, where I was first turned under

I know the room you sleep in
Is circled by horses
Their curved flanks quivering, their necks
Like rivers, an unbearable pungence
Illumines my sentence

Stars hung in the usual night
Blink aroused.

Foretold

So I arrive
uncircumcised of heart unto
your body's landscape, marvelous,
its lean parts straining
to become visible
at the start of a concentration
that would impose
itself like a forehead
against a rough wall.
Nor is that all
that can be said.
The thinnest emerald
and red motes drift
slantwise through this
startling light, expose
the possibility I might well
hold it in my mouth
and speak it to you, enter
your dark with my tongue,
the palestine of your mysteries
which increase like a sum
of our breath. My reader
looks over my shoulder
as I write.

Flatwoods

Once there was another state
and I lived there.
I remember farting across the bridge
to your apartment
like a toy train.
Christmas, the day I gave up,
it was shining everywhere
on account of the rain.
Sometimes, when I see two
egrets disturbed by the sun
which is torching the delta's edge,
I do not recall my emptiness. I think,
There go two birds, so what. Fly to hell.

Norfolk

From across the room, its clutter
of voices, I can tell it is you
who has called us long distance.
Don't ask me how.
Your absence is my slow,
painful disintoxication.
Things I would say
if you asked for me.

Once, before my attic filled with owls,
I laid my head on your belly
and listened to your childhood,
a girl leading the white
bull to the fields. In sleep
you spoke, but the word was drowsy,
I didn't understand it.
Into your hair I mouthed your name,
into your body's lovely neck.
And I thought, then, there was some limit
to set on my pain.

Garden of Cucumbers

River smell
behind your ear and
cold-
tipped fingers.
The rural
landscape in your eyes
lingers. Hold me
in them as
I you, mouth
too, to
speak of
me.

Everyone Can't Be an Orphan

Beyond, the vinous bikers dismount.
We walk the river
past dehiscent seedpods, a line of buttonwood trees
beaming with river
light, and the sun goes.
Your hairless belly guiding my volant touch.
In our quiet, we agree
to the dialect and the gestuary
we would occupy.
The bridge view comes on, and
our particularly intimate form of pioneering.
You grasp everything immediately.
My thumb tracing armpit and slow
curve to your waist,
the osage orange losing its bees.
Every future is complete without us.
Like the Giottos at Padua. We
emerge as a vocabulary
febrile and ardent blue.

Epithalamium

Whatever you think I've done
hasn't killed you.
So shut up.
Your friends have gone
like the northern constellations.
Your friends have left you
with me, I leave you
the same. Open your lips,
husband. If I thought I would drain
the murky bath of your sadness,
I watched you instead
slip into the water
without your glasses.
You are so white
like polished wood, poised
like William and Mary chairs.
You know quite a lot,
but not about me.
Follow now
to the bedroom with my nakedness
the only light.

Guest Quarters

Gauze curtains
billowing into room
before storm.
Lawn mower kicks,
sticks, cuts off
in mint below window.
Sputters into hum again.
Stepladder in back-
yard on either side
of high rock fence,
scolding wrens.
Then, you knock twice,
come in.
My balls rise.

The Tapestry

—for Pilar Coover

Me, when I think of you I see
Alley cats in your kitchen,
God weeping at your openings,
Individual acts of imagination, never
Culligan men under

Floorboards slipping hallucinogens into your water.
Let me say I have imagined you
Undressing guests before mirrors
To let their dragonfly bodies
Escape from human shells.

The Man Who Won't Pay Dues

While the bad slept well, he
moiled, sweating, on the sofa.

Telephone, she sings from the kitchen
as he pops the hood.
Their daughter stamping swarms
of ants into dust. The man
considers his stalled Ford,
his Adam's apple rising
and falling. The hound wails,
the girl pulls down her panties
by the tottering clothesline.

Sock-footed, he pivots on the stoop
and a splinter goes deep.
The screen door slams
next to a chevron of sand
she has swept beside his Red Wings.

Draft of the Smoky Life

As the store windows light up
in the downhearted district
where children are never seen,
men collect at The Town Pump,
our faces orange in the sunset,
each of us holding out
the meat of his hand to be stamped
as though to register
our stand against oblivion.

Tracking our reflection
in long mirrors, keeping our appointment
to be cured in smoke.

We sit on fingers
nicked by tools
watching the thighs
of dancers. Our
legs wrap around
chair legs, roads
come down the mountain.
Into the curves each man
tailgates his desire.
But each man tailgates the same
desire. When we enter here

something falls through us
from out of a blue hope.

The air blurred and hoarse,
we get freaky with our own smell,

our flannel shirts stink to hell
of hung fire and beer.

There is no band. We go
into the men's room holding hands.

Sickness

When I thought I was testing you
    I was leaving you,
      watching to see if you'd save me.

During this time, I died
    of cold, white cold,
      turds dogs wouldn't sniff.
    I thought I had died,
      I felt so sorry for myself.

You twisted the washcloth
      between your hands over a basin
      scraped in some places blue as
          bullets.
      You laid it on my forehead
          gently.

The History of My People

Tired of being a man,
I slept one afternoon fully dressed
with the radio hissing like a swan,
and dreamed I was a woman
traveling through another country
with a caravan of strangers and dromedaries
trailing long silk swatches in the foehn
from packs hung with wineskins and bags of candied fruit,
date wine and tobacco leaves.
My eyes were going bad under the sun,
I kept falling behind.
Sometimes the camels disappeared in waves of heat
and then I would follow their dung trail
sweetly stinking.
My legs were so muscled and brown,
a horseman appeared. He scooped
me up and I straddled the raspy mane,
my robes blowing out behind us
like the tail of Nebuchadnezzar's peacock.
As we flew toward the caravan
I gulped hot wind, kneading my thighs
against the animal's neck
to keep from falling. Inside my belly
children awakened.

Psychoanalysis of Water

The clock here is quiet.
Into the rain's applause,
a woman rises
fatigued. Tablets
dissolve in a glass by the bed.
The wind lifts, branches
animating inconsonant darkness.
She undoes her gown,
lays it over the bedpost.
Seductive leg hair. Almost
dawn, she makes coffee like that.

Low thunder, glints
of lightning, the dog's
concern. *Rain on the roof,*
friends walking across my grave,
her mother told her, *that's all*
I listen for.
And why not the hiss and wake
of cars on the wet road
bursting into transparence under tents
of streetlight, winking out
into afterglow. Glances that catch
anonymous faces at windows
in early lit houses like her own.

This way she drifts off, mesmerically.
The bathtub overflowing.

III. Life of Johnson Upside Your Head, *a Libretto*

Came down along the road carrying his Stella
guitar like a misshapen child on his back,

And stood at the side in dog fennel to watch the hearse
he'd heard for half a mile bottoming out on the rutted road,
sucking up a tunnel of dust in its wake, dust to dust,

Approacheth and fishtaileth on toward Protho Junction.

He passes into that cloud.

She who turns old boards
in the dirt for worms
        peers through the blue bottle
                tree as he strolls past.
                Holds his glare. Elms there
        whitewashed to beyond his reach,
                        ragged hens. The glabrous hog shrieking.
                So he goes. His own
                        steady footfall reverberant
                in the verdurous undergrowth.
        At either side,
the sandy road impinged upon
                by stumps rotten and flowered
                                with fungus. His palms
                flashing behind him.
        Before he arrives,
                        tramps beat the proprietor from his store
                        force him through the outhouse hole,
                cotton prices decline, neighbors
                                to the suck hole
                roll the drowned schoolboy over
                a log and revive him.
                                Full sun. Bitterweed
on his tongue.
        In the distant field
                        two hanging figures, cattle
                standing below in a stare.

That it was evening because the west had gone red
and the chiggers had increased in his wrists.
From the flatbed he could see
a girl in a knee-length dress holding her hands
on top of her head, her face framed;
laundry staying out late.
He loved his sister's skin.
As though he could blow on it and it would riffle.
How drinking shoe polish strained through white bread
lodged a peckerwood behind their brains.
Their father was soaking half a cooked chicken in Paris Green,
kneading in some Rough on Rats,
and limping out to find the mongrel
under the drugstore porch. Then the rumor:
he couldn't no way have been their father.
The boy claimed, Two people
are inside me. A brother learned taxidermy
from a book. He played harp in the outhouse.
When you sit in the outhouse a while
you begin to imagine bad things
live in the shit and right this moment
they are looking up at your butt
getting an idea.
He married young.

At the time I met him
the so-called guitar player was fresh
out of Memphis, thumb out
where the roads crossed
and I thought he must have been teenage.
But he didn't like that
title of being kid. Was a man
far as he was concerned.

I said, Now son, forget that
motion picture left hand, good evening,
my name is Tush Hog.
He said, I pick cotton for no man
and I ain't skeared of you Satan.

She had looked in the crib
to see a brown
        recluse   pulsing
           on her baby's forehead.

One of the cross
      staves supporting the coffin
broke,
   so that it plunged
         forward, splintering open.

Between Calvary
      Baptist Church Parsonage and the grave-
  yard, the reverend's planking
addressed a muddy washout

         and the women in their meeting clothes
         walked over this now
  single file, their heads tilted
    down.

He arrived of an evening
        in a suit covered with road. Rags hung
   burning
    in a corner, for the mosquitoes
 were bad. She let go
        a kettle of hot water, smoothed
        calico skirt to the backs of her knees.
Hilo, Dusty, she answered.

The Devil hummed around the tonic, the blue third and the fifth
he snatched this out of air
to cock it on the wall, controlling timbre
while planters *prastered off like a load of bokros*

Smashes the sound box with his palm
sheep went astray the moon shot an octave
a cruel glare floods his skull his voice
tinkered with a picker biting a raw yellow onion

Then screws up slab of face
distorting linear time severing brambles
and readjusts his mouth cavity
takes off his jacket to reveal a downpour

The Devil intimated to make a long piss short
he slides tone around axis dragging limp bags
through cotton fields railing in embers on levee chipped
tooth doing jake leg and yawns tin can over
what young plant awaiting the revenant's
hallelujah immersed in 1932 brief, mosquito-bitten, gone.

In the night he rose
and came out to piss.
The moon smoldered like a burnt tick.
Turning inside,
he stepped on something he thought
was a clump of hair, a wolf
spider with her ball of children
whose thousands spilled
over his bare foot.

We'd be on the road for days
  and days sidestepping copperheads,
   waylaid by noisome crows
    and buntings chasing us along
     fences, kick up the dust,
      I'm checking his head for ticks, June bugs
       squeak like bad wheels, sleeping off
        under bodarks with our guitars
         lying up and down our breast
         talking about women and him
        imitating goatsuckers, no money, then
          come into town with gnats mashed in our eye
          and see nice posters for picnics

          and band concerts and we'd play
            on dusty streets or inside dirty places
           of the sort you played in those times,
             a couple stuffed raccoons in a corner, fried
             tripe stinking to high heaven, field hands
            screwing their heads on backways
          of a Saturday night, and somebody
        might fall through the door laughing
         with two or three rat snakes
         strangulating his arms and neck, I'd go
    get a cool drink, come back
       with splinters, rubbing up against how many
    women says she'll squeeze my lcmon for fifty
      cents and I'd catch my breath
        and see myself looking purely
         like a three-legged dog, there he'd be
     all clean as can be, looking like
       he's just stepped out of church.

I would just as lief you go alone, she answered.
Grinding coffee beans, dipping
a cup in the water bucket four times
to fill the porcelain pot.
Hot as a two-peckered goat. Morning.
The weight of her coppled breast.
Accused of burglary, pleading somnambulism.
The road was two deep ruts on either side
of a big hump. Misery runs on a broken leash.
As when the hypnotist says so, he remembered.
Shot herself while looking in a mirror.
One photograph: their infant in a coffin.
The Sliding Delta outside his door
in Tunica County, Mississippi, near the cemetery at Three Forks.

He cannot breathe
Wearing gloves, goes bare-handed
On bitterest evenings.

The voice the dead man's voice is young and tight and high
the naturalness of it as language a man's voice
tuned a little sharp the image of the voice
a pressured high and letting out
the dead man's falsetto counterpointing a drum beat
in lower register his guitar breathing the blinds
of syllables his chair squeaks voice undulating
outside the wire-thin loops of swallows in his voice
the diphtheria epidemic in his voice the barn fires
his father a drunk in the dark
mistaking carbolic acid for cough medicine
bottleneck slide groups of triplets
in the treble strings tuned sharp thumb
for hard rhythm intensity inside him his mouth
a little slack the concentration inside
the voice an orphan who ate match heads
his wife on the cooling board his baby buried
pain's medium voice contours of landscape eroded
mortal erotic upwelling to warp as the degree
of emotion the power to be funny
jammed through oblivion like crowbar cotton
fields frog gig pissing in wild sweet peas
sweat lubricating voice sex speeding up the dead
man's voice orphaned from its mouth

Came to St. Louis a stranger and heard Henry Townsend hustling a small crowd by the train station. Listened a bit, then said, "Look, I've heard about you. Where you playing tonight. Can I come over?"

In fact, Townsend had a regular evening gig at Ernest Walker's house party on Jefferson. Walking around the Nickel, working at a toothache with his tongue, he occasionally stopped to write something down in a flat black notebook he carried in his trousers. He watched out for the police. There at the side of Black Cats Drugstore, he was entangled in a game of pitch and stayed until he noticed bull bats overhead. Then he picked up his guitar, told everybody he was due at Ernest Walker's house party where he was musicianing tonight and they should all come on over.

Townsend was tuning up in the backyard when he sat down next to him and proceeded to go over some guitar. Townsend's eyes glowed dimly. He thought, This guy has it. He's amazing.

Long tables out back and dogs
everywhere, maybe seventy people
slapping tables or winging bones
at the animals. Women
and men both lying around in bushes
on all sides dethroned
of their reason, or dancing. Thighs
in ceaseless friction.
Sweat washing all of them,
night sweat, clothing soaked, sterno sweat, blind
faces glowing like a new shoe shine
and he, set up precariously
in a chair on a frequently bumped table,
wearing a brand new fedora, eyes
hooded by his brow,
playing guitar with a broken bottleneck
and his left hand fingers bleeding across the strings.

He is still getting clear high notes,
still getting drunker, when a mulatto
on a bet wrestles down a pariah dog
and his friend pours a full lantern
of coal oil over it then touches a match
to its tail whereupon
half the first man and all the dog

instantly blow up, visions of hell each
howling and burning a brief passageway
through stumbling bodies toward the street.

You'd have radio
songs on he'd be long
in the tooth talking
note for note
thinking
to you
out of that idea
he was just having

1. Wood bench barrel on side two chair sunk
   veranda Mose Brown's Dry Goods semi-
   retired men one soak feet bucket epsom salt water.

2. Came town man electric machine you see what
   was crank phone two wire come out he start
   poker dealer voice soon decent crowd. Some mischief
   unharness his standing team, boys. Nickel
   bet how long Snead Noe his feet that bucket once crank.

3. Look serious like take shit. Car come boy shout everyone
   turn head Intermediary Christ Snead Noe rip pant barrel cinch
   head hit wall rock back splash bucket water. Dust devil follow car
   pull up Drugstore and Lemonade. Mischief hang back then
   surround car, boys.

4. White man slam door step butterfly cover horse dung kick
   porch enter store cough three time proprietor most deaf read
   magazine swat fly man cough heart attack proprietor raise head
   lower glasses boys open door Snead Noe shout across street
   I'm looking for a guitar player name of, white man says. What.

5. Across street other man smile put feet bucket water nickel bet
   Sneed Noe shake head white man look get car back horse dung
   butterfly electric crank machine men whoop car shift first
   grind white man see last eight hundred pound hog boy lead
   string knock house door open huge testicle too big fit under
   hog out squeeze behind leg two watermelon tail open wide
   door go boy string hog. Goddamn.

A time in St. Louis
we were playing one of the songs
that he'd like to play once
in a great while.

He was playing very slow
and passionate
and when we quit
I noticed no one
was saying anything. Then
I saw they were all crying,
both women and men.

He ends here, a sort of omen. History accelerates. The excluded remains to disrupt the structures that would domesticate it. Unimproved, his voice turns away at the most intense moments of emotion. Into grooves. You bloodless and attenuated: here is the rufous prophet wailing a blue fuck. The prompt sound. Where the Mississippi embouchures. Sixty years ago, a voice that no longer exists in a room that no longer exists. Fugitive tendency. Erotic disorder. He woke up this morning and reached under the bed for his shoes. Material added by way of analogy. I lacks a nickel. The barber who clipped his nose hairs. When you get down to the lick log. Ruminations of sex without love, love without children. Undergrowth with two figures. Part of his earlobe torn off in a married woman's teeth. Pubic hairs shed in the beds of strangers. Ass curve moonlight. Stared into landscapes in ceilings, knots and their tributaries and lead-based paint unfolding moth wings. Reeling stars. Bulge in his pants at her funeral. Instead of a country a set of traps. There is not much time in the day between death and life. Tuning. His dogs, throat eaters, untamed and invisible. A weed under tongue. Wanted to be a living man.

About the Author

FORREST GANDER was born in 1956 and grew up in Virginia with his mother and sisters. In 1972 his mother met and married Walter J. Gander, a widower with two sons. Adopted, Forrest Gander attended The College of William and Mary where he double majored in geology and English in 1978. In 1980 he drove to San Francisco to study poetry, graduating from San Francisco State University with a master's degree. From there, he and poet C. D. Wright lived in Mexico, in the Ozarks of Arkansas, and now, with a child, in Rhode Island where Gander keeps an orchard and makes his living as an associate professor of English at Providence College. Together, Gander and Wright coedit Lost Roads Publishers, a literary book press.

Pitt Poetry Series
Ed Ochester, General Editor